CONTENTS

Published on December 30, 2013.

Suggested Citation:

Antos, M., Kenefick, A., and Steele, N. *Disadvantaged Community Outreach Evaluation Study: An Analysis Of Technical Assistance And Outreach Methods*. Los Angeles: Council for Watershed Health, 2013.

SUMMARY OF FINDINGS & RECOMMENDATIONS

This Disadvantaged Community Outreach Evaluation study was completed under an agreement between the Council for Watershed Health (Council) and the California Department of Water Resources (DWR) with funding from Proposition 84: The Safe Drinking Water, Water Quality and Supply, Flood Control, River and Coastal Protection Bond Act of 2006. Additional assistance was provided by the Greater Los Angeles County Integrated Regional Water Management (GLAC-IRWM) group and Los Angeles County Flood Control District, which provided in-kind technical assistance via an agreement with the United States Army Corps of Engineers (USACE) Planning Assistance to the States program. The Council conducted the study on behalf of the GLAC-IRWM group and with the assistance of the GLAC-IRWM Disadvantaged Community committee.

The study worked to unpack the assumptions embedded in previous Disadvantaged Community (DAC) outreach efforts. First, we asked if the system of identifying disadvantaged communities was effective. We found that US Census tracts, which are commonly used to designate the boundaries of DAC, are very poor at properly describing communities. Second, we considered the implications of the single-indicator system (median-household income) for identifying and understanding disadvantaged communities. We found that this system is not sufficient; additional indicators we determined are necessary to characterize a community include the *size* of each community, and the *uniformity* and *intensity* of the disadvantage experienced by members of each community. We developed a multi-indicator assessment tool that helps better describe each disadvantaged community so that engagement efforts can be properly designed.

Using the tools we developed to identify and understand communities, we conducted needs assessments and targeted outreach to engage members of five disadvantaged communities. These efforts facilitated participation of community members in the integrated water management (IWM) process. The needs assessment and outreach resulted in twenty-two of project concepts appropriate for IWM funding. Of those concepts, eight received technical assistance to fully develop project concept reports.

The study resulted in findings and recommendations for improving the engagement of members of disadvantaged communities, specifically for urban areas but which are also likely applicable statewide:

Indicators of Disadvantage. Properly identifying and understanding a disadvantaged community greatly improves efforts to engage with its members. The use of the median-household income statistic has utility, however it is not sufficient when developing an engagement strategy that relies on awareness of a community's individuality.

We recommend that DWR invest in research to enhance and expand the tools created here that provides IWM groups with the information necessary to properly identify community boundaries and to help understand the *uniformity* and *intensity* of the disadvantage experienced by each community.

Investment in Communities. Engagement requires particular skills and the investment of both time and money. Funding directed towards people and organizations with necessary skills is required for IWM agencies to conduct effective and sustainable disadvantaged community engagement.

We recommend that DWR use grant guidelines to create a set-aside, perhaps up to 10 percent, within planning grants for engagement activities. Grantees should enunciate an engagement plan to access these targeted planning funds and the resources used to assure disadvantaged community members are able to participate in IWM planning efforts.

Orienting Towards Results. Members of disadvantaged communities and the organizations most able to engage on water issues struggle to use state grant funds themselves because of the long period between incurring an expense and receiving reimbursement. To overcome this challenge, we provided our outreach contractors up-front money to permit them to accomplish tasks they were otherwise unable to perform for lack of operating funds.

We recommend that DWR make it easier for small agencies and organizations to conduct this work through expedited reimbursement and small up-front funding grants.

Synergistic Coordination. In urban Southern California, the work of watershed coordinators and the work of disadvantaged community outreach are very similar. DWR and IWM would benefit by aligning with the California Department of Conservation to provide additional resources, goals, and agency support for the Watershed Coordination Program.

We recommend DWR work with DOC to strengthen and expand the Watershed Coordination Program in highly-urbanized areas to leverage a successful and existing program, which is currently underfunded and understaffed.

Critical Needs. Urban and rural disadvantaged communities have different critical needs within the IWM scope and must be considered using different metrics. No critical need is "more" than another; instead each is unique to the context of a particular community.

We recommend that DWR broaden its guidance on 'critical needs' to include the water-related challenges of urban disadvantaged communities including: flood hazards, drinking water quality, stormwater quality, and lack of open space.

Inclusiveness and Sensitivity. The concept of "disadvantaged community" is a powerful tool, defined in policy documents, California Codes, and bond language. Care must be taken during engagement with people so that their lived experience is acknowledged and respected. The reductionist nature of the name (and particularly the pronounced acronym "Dacks") can work to reaffirm barriers and differences between the parties in an engagement.

We recommend that DWR work with appropriate experts in communications and community members to develop conscientious language and guidance that improves the inclusiveness and sensitivity of engagement efforts.

INTRODUCTION TO THE STUDY

This Disadvantaged Community Outreach Evaluation Study (Study) was completed under an agreement between the Council for Watershed Health (Council) and the California Department of Water Resources (DWR) with funding from Proposition 84: The Safe Drinking Water, Water Quality and Supply, Flood Control, River and Coastal Protection Bond Act of 2006. The Council conducted the study on behalf of the Greater Los Angeles County regional water management group, which also contributed funding. The Los Angeles County Flood Control District provided in-kind technical assistance via an agreement with the United States Army Corps of Engineers (USACE) Planning Assistance to the States program.

The Study had two primary goals: to develop tools for understanding the diversity of challenges and characteristics of the communities in the region and to identify critically needed projects in each of the five subregions of the Greater Los Angeles County Integrated Regional Water Management (GLAC-IRWM) region. In order to accomplish these goals, we devised a regional needs assessment framework, a mixed qualitative and quantitative method for assessing community boundaries, and a multi-indicator assessment framework for understanding the challenges faced by each individual community. We engaged with five communities in the GLAC-IRWM region and provided technical support to five agencies for project development.

In 2009, the GLAC-IRWM was asked by DWR to develop a proposal for a DAC outreach evaluation research project. The GLAC leadership committee requested the Council for Watershed Health, a member of the leadership and DAC committees, to develop the proposal and then conduct the work of the grant. The Council worked with members of the leadership and DAC committees to draft the funding proposal, with the DAC committee serving as a technical advisory committee for the Study.

The grant was awarded in December 2011, and has been extended once to conclude December 2013. The GLAC Leadership Committee supplied a 10% match, resulting in a total budget of $550,000. The additional work completed by US Army Corps of Engineers is valued at $450,000.

DISADVANTAGED COMMUNITIES OF GREATER LOS ANGELES COUNTY

The region served by the GLAC-IRWM is unique in California. According to the 2010 US Census, 26% of all Californians live here, and 41% of those living in the region are residents of a disadvantaged community census tract. Statewide, one-third of all Californians who live in disadvantaged community census tracts live in the GLAC region *(Figure 1)*. Though DWR has acknowledged that census tracts, census places, and census block groups are available geographic boundaries for designating DAC, this study uses only census tracts as the appropriate scale for the regional assessment and statewide comparisons.

The GLAC-IRWM region is densely developed, with 88 cities as well as unincorporated Los Angeles County, and hundreds of public agencies and private companies with water management authority or responsibility. The institutional and population density express both the scale of the challenge, but also the extent to which improvement will bring benefits to Californians. IWM capacity engaged in the communities of GLAC-IRWM can potentially improve millions of lives.

Outreach to communities can be challenging for IWM agencies. Often contact between agency staff and the public is managed through elected boards and representatives, or handled directly only through billing or mailed outreach material. Disadvantaged communities often lack connections to formal networks and civic institutions. IWM agencies need assistance to bring the appropriate capacity to bear on the challenge of engaging with disadvantaged communities.

IWM projects require significant technical knowledge to design. Community groups, even active non-profit organizations, rarely have resources or staff capable of the engineering. Providing technical support to bring project concepts created by communities through the IWM process to compete for resources is a necessary component of disadvantaged community engagement.

Figure 1. Population statistics by DAC tracts and the Greater Los Angeles County - Integrated Regional Water Management area (GLAC-IRWM)

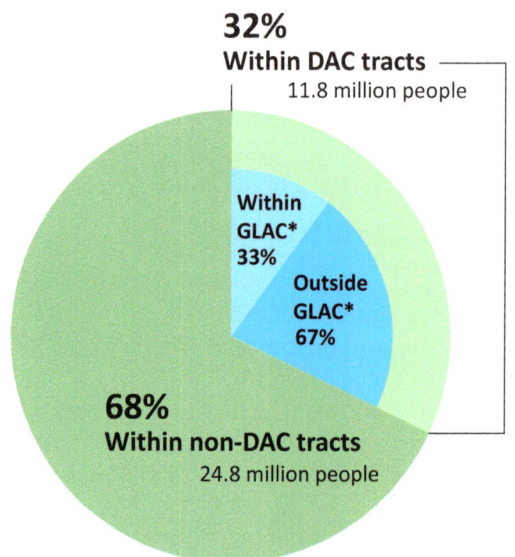

CALIFORNIA POPULATION
Each circle represents 36.6 million people

32%
Within DAC tracts
11.8 million people

Within GLAC* 33%

Outside GLAC* 67%

68%
Within non-DAC tracts
24.8 million people

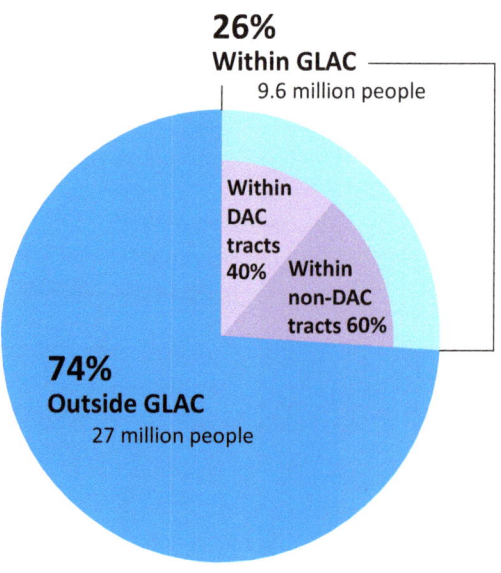

26%
Within GLAC
9.6 million people

Within DAC tracts 40%

Within non-DAC tracts 60%

74%
Outside GLAC
27 million people

* Greater Los Angeles County IRWM Area

Brief History of DAC Outreach in GLAC

In 2008, the GLAC-IRWM leadership committee formed an ad-hoc committee to develop an outreach plan for disadvantaged communities. The resulting interim outreach plan acknowledged that meaningful public participation is critical when setting goals, objectives, and strategies to bring benefits to a community. The plan proposed the following outreach process:

• Use a phased approach to implement the outreach plan, gradually reaching more people living and working in the region's disadvantaged communities with water resource issues.

• In the near-term, given the resources available from the IWM process, work with disadvantaged communities to further develop projects from the current IWM Plan projects list, providing technical support and helping communities identify leads, funding sources, and other resources.

• Over time, work with identified disadvantaged communities and their representatives to develop a comprehensive analysis of the water-related needs of these communities throughout the region.

• Also over time, as additional resources are available to the IWM process, work with disadvantaged communities to develop a suite of projects to address the identified needs and include them in the IRWM Plan.

The leadership committee adopted the plan in October 2008, identifying "outreach to disadvantaged communities as one of [the GLAC-IRWM leadership committee's] highest priorities." The plan recognizes that outreach must be conducted at the sub-regional steering committee level but that resources were not available to fund much of the work.

TIMELINE AND SUMMARY OF GLAC-IRWM DISADVANTAGED COMMUNITY EFFORTS

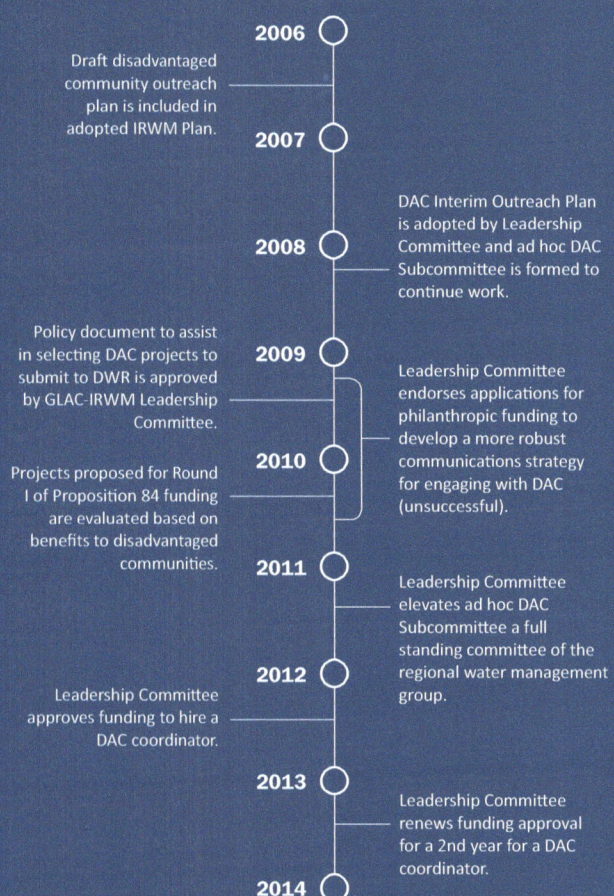

2006

Draft disadvantaged community outreach plan is included in adopted IRWM Plan.

2007

DAC Interim Outreach Plan is adopted by Leadership Committee and ad hoc DAC Subcommittee is formed to continue work.

2008

Policy document to assist in selecting DAC projects to submit to DWR is approved by GLAC-IRWM Leadership Committee.

2009

Leadership Committee endorses applications for philanthropic funding to develop a more robust communications strategy for engaging with DAC (unsuccessful).

Projects proposed for Round I of Proposition 84 funding are evaluated based on benefits to disadvantaged communities.

2010

2011

Leadership Committee elevates ad hoc DAC Subcommittee a full standing committee of the regional water management group.

Leadership Committee approves funding to hire a DAC coordinator.

2012

2013

Leadership Committee renews funding approval for a 2nd year for a DAC coordinator.

2014

The interim outreach plan acknowledged that engagement with members of disadvantaged communities had been insufficient to achieve meaningful input in the development of projects. Although projects benefiting disadvantaged communities were regularly proposed, and some were successful in receiving funding by agencies serving these communities, these projects have all been generated from "top-down" planning. Thus, the GLAC-IRWM requested that California Department of Water Resources (DWR) make funding available to increase the level of community member participation in project development, and to improve local capacity to perform successful engagement efforts.

PROCESS OF THE STUDY

Identifying Disadvantaged Communities

It is critical to be certain that a community where engagement efforts are proposed is a coherent community that will respond to the effort. How people self-identify as members of communities can be complex in urban regions such as Greater Los Angeles County.

Perceived boundaries are often unrelated to political or administrative boundaries. Because of the legal framework of "disadvantaged communities" in IWM, US Census boundaries are frequently used to designate community boundaries. Grant guidelines reference the California Water Code and Public Resources Code, where disadvantaged communities are measured by their median household income as compared to the statewide median household income (MHI). The US Census reports MHI within their geographic boundaries. These census boundaries were not developed to identify communities, and therefore do it poorly.

The process of identifying a community is critical to engaging with the community. Limiting analyses to census tracts also limits the ability to place good projects and artificially limits the "beneficiaries" to those in the same tract. The nature of the "disadvantage" faced is rarely similar from one community to the next. Using MHI to differentiate between two categories ("disadvantaged" and "not disadvantaged") poorly resolves the challenges particular communities face, and provides very little information to those seeking to engage with the community. One goal of the research described below was identifying other indicators that express the individuality of each community.

US Census geographic boundaries serve the purposes of the Census as function-based geographical units and often fail to describe the true nature of communities[1]. In the urban space of Southern California, tracts do not appropriately define communities. Political boundaries, language, physical barriers, and transportation pathways are examples of the influences that impact how people perceive their place in a community.

The project team used desktop analysis and field surveys to draw the boundaries of communities within the GLAC-IRWM region. This process involved each contractor and the Council's watershed coordination staff pouring over a US census tract map of the region, combining tracts, slicing some and omitting others. Multiple other neighborhood classifications[2] were referenced, including the Los Angeles Times neighborhood project[3], real-estate websites[4], and observation-based data[5]. Freeways, railways and waterways lacking bridges or underpasses were considered as barriers. Paths, nodes, landmarks and other elements that directed traffic and activity were also explored as potential community foci. The 954 DAC tracts identified by the 2010 Census in the region, once processed, resulted in 109 disadvantaged communities.

Each new amalgam community was given a place-holder name, and then reprocessed through the MHI statistic as a "community". *Figure 2* displays these communities[6]. In some cases, a community would include tracts that themselves are not under the MHI threshold, but because of neighboring tracts in the same community are under the MHI threshold, the entire community is considered a disadvantaged community. In no case was a DAC tract not considered part of a resulting disadvantaged community.

Understanding Disadvantage

Properly understanding the individualized characteristics of each disadvantaged community improves engagement efforts. One example characteristic that is commonly used is median-household income; MHI, however, is not sufficient when developing an engagement strategy that relies on awareness of a community's individuality. Prior to engagement, discovering the "disadvantage" in a particular community can be instructive in the design of the engagement process.

1   Dietz, Robert D. 2002. "The Estimation of Neighborhood Effects in the Social Sciences: an Interdisciplinary Approach." Social Science Research 31 (4): 539–575.

2   http://zimas.lacity.org

3   http://projects.latimes.com/mapping-la/neighborhoods

4   http://www.zillow.com

5   Lynch, Kevin. *The Image of the City.* 1960, MIT Press, p 46-85.

6   An online dynamic map with these geographies is available at http://wc.watershedhealth.org

Figure 2. Disadvantaged Communities Map

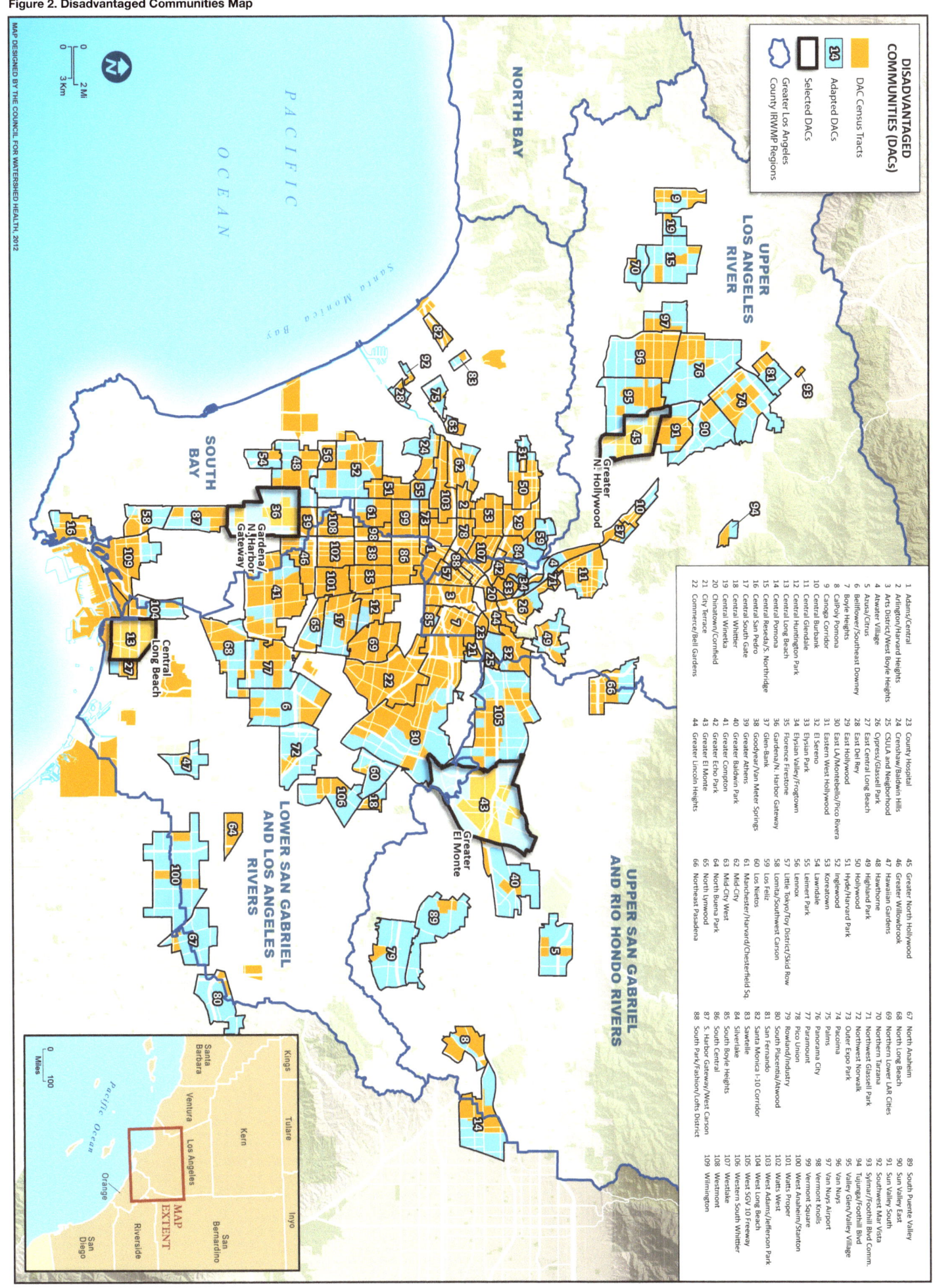

DISADVANTAGED COMMUNITIES (DACs)

- DAC Census Tracts
- 14 Adapted DACs
- Selected DACs
- Greater Los Angeles County IRWMP Regions

1 Adams/Central	23 County Hospital
2 Arlington/Harvard Heights	24 Crenshaw/Baldwin Hills
3 Arts District/West Boyle Heights	25 CSULA and Neighborhood
4 Atwater Village	26 Cypress/Glassell Park
5 Azusa/Citrus	27 East Central Long Beach
6 Bellflower/Southeast Downey	28 East Del Rey
7 Boyle Heights	29 East Hollywood
8 CalPoly Pomona	30 East LA/Montebello/Pico Rivera
9 Canoga Corridor	31 Eastern West Hollywood
10 Central Burbank	32 El Sereno
11 Central Glendale	33 Elysian Park
12 Central Huntington Park	34 Elysian Valley/Frogtown
13 Central Long Beach	35 Florence Firestone
14 Central Pomona	36 Gardena/N. Harbor Gateway
15 Central Reseda/S. Northridge	37 Glen-Bank
16 Central San Pedro	38 Goodyear/Van Meter Springs
17 Central South Gate	39 Greater Athens
18 Central Whittier	40 Greater Baldwin Park
19 Central Winetka	41 Greater Compton
20 Chinatown/Cornfield	42 Greater Echo Park
21 City Terrace	43 Greater El Monte
22 Commerce/Bell Gardens	44 Greater Lincoln Heights

45 Greater North Hollywood	67 North Anaheim
46 Greater Willowbrook	68 North Long Beach
47 Hawaiian Gardens	69 Northern Lower LAR Cities
48 Hawthorne	70 Southwest Mar Vista
49 Highland Park	71 Northwest Glassell Park
50 Hollywood	72 Northwest Norwalk
51 Hyde/Harvard Park	73 Outer Expo Park
52 Inglewood	74 Pacoima
53 Koreatown	75 Palms
54 Lawndale	76 Panorama City
55 Leimert Park	77 Paramount
56 Lennox	78 Pico Union
57 Little Tokyo/Toy District/Skid Row	79 Rowland/Industry
58 Lomita/Southwest Carson	80 South Placentia/Atwood
59 Los Feliz	81 San Fernando
60 Los Nietos	82 Santa Monica I-10 Corridor
61 Manchester/Harvard/Chesterfield Sq.	83 Sawtelle
62 Mid-City	84 Silverlake
63 Mid-City West	85 South Boyle Heights
64 North Buena Park	86 South Central
65 North Lynwood	87 S. Harbor Gateway/West Carson
66 Northeast Pasadena	88 South Park/Fashion/Lofts District

89 South Puente Valley
90 Sun Valley East
91 Sun Valley South
92 Southwest Mar Vista
93 Sylmar/Foothill Blvd Comm.
94 Tujunga/Foothill Blvd
95 Valley Glen/Valley Village
96 Van Nuys
97 Van Nuys Airport
98 Vermont Knolls
99 Vermont Square
100 West Anaheim/Stanton
101 Watts Proper
102 Watts West
103 West Adams/Jefferson Park
104 West Long Beach
105 West SGV 10 Freeway
106 Western South Whittier
107 Westlake
108 Westmont
109 Wilmington

PACIFIC OCEAN

Santa Monica Bay

NORTH BAY

UPPER LOS ANGELES RIVER

SOUTH BAY

Greater N. Hollywood

Gardena/ N. Harbor Gateway

Central Long Beach

LOWER SAN GABRIEL AND LOS ANGELES RIVERS

Greater El Monte

UPPER SAN GABRIEL AND RIO HONDO RIVERS

0 2 Mi
0 3 Km

MAP EXTENT

Santa Barbara | Kings | Tulare | Inyo
Ventura | Kern
Pacific Ocean | Los Angeles | San Bernardino
Orange
San Diego | Riverside

0 100 Miles

Table 1. Indicators used to understand disadvantaged communities.

	Indicator	Higher Score	Lower Score
Size	Population	Higher population	Lower population
Uniformity	Park access	Some or all residents have poor access	All residents have good access
	Percentage of residents whose individual households meet the DAC threshold	Closer to 100%	Closer to 50%
	Percentage of home owners	Lower number	Higher number
Intensity	Median household income	Lower number	Higher number
	Median household rent	Higher percentage of MHI	Lower percentage of MHI
	Population turnover	Higher percentage	Lower percentage
	Educational attainment	Highest dropout rate	Lowest dropout rate
	Unemployment	Highest unemployment	Lower unemployment

The Study developed a multi-indicator analysis of available data to help understand communities *(Table 1)*. Using the community boundaries developed by the study, a suite of indicators was analyzed to describe the *size* of each community, and the *intensity* and *uniformity* of the challenges faced by the community.

SIZE

This index included only one indicator – population. Knowing how many people are within the community helps frame the engagement effort. It also describes the potential benefits of proposed project.

UNIFORMITY

The index of uniformity measures how many households in the community are experiencing the same conditions. Where challenges are felt uniformly the community will respond differently to engagement than in a community where challenges are variable in their impact. The three uniformity indicators are:

• **Park Access.** This indicator used a spatial analysis to describe the percentage of people in each community are within ¼ mile of a park. Access to open space is called out in the GLAC-IRWM plan as a goal that can achieve multiple benefits. The analysis used census block level data and Southern California Area Governments land-use data to classify each block with or without access to a park. Blocks were summed to each selected community to

calculate what percentage of the community population had access. This indicator was scored to show how uniformly the residents of the community are experiencing poor or no access to parks.

• **Household Income.** This indicator relies on Census data to reveal the percentage of households in the community that are below the DAC MHI threshold. A high level of uniformity means that most households are low-income and a low level of uniformity means that the community has a mixture of low- and middle- or high-income households.

• **Home Ownership.** It is conventional wisdom that increasing home-ownership can stabilize areas in decline[7]. A community with a predominance of homeowners will engage with an effort differently than will one with mostly renters. This challenge appeared during the pilot engagement effort in Maywood, where most community members who worked with us are renters, claiming their owners are distant from the city and disengaged. This statistic was calculated to show a community with less homeownership as being more uniformly disadvantaged.

---

7   Homeownership and Neighborhood Stability; Housing Policy Debate; Volume 7, Issue I, p. 37; Fannie Mae Foundation 1996. Available: *http://content.knowledgeplex.org/kp2/img/cache/documents/1373.pdf*

INTENSITY

This index seeks to describe the extent of the challenges felt in the community. Understanding how much capacity there is in a community to engage is a necessary first step analysis. In communities at the extremes, the need for specific forms of engagement, or the special attention for project development, can be observed through this analysis. The model used five indicators of intensity:

- **Median Household Income**. Each community was found to be under the state-mandated MHI. This indicator ranked these disadvantaged communities using the MHI statistic, with the lowest MHIs having the highest *intensity*.

- **Household Rent**. In communities where more income is consumed by housing costs, there is less capacity to participate in other aspects of civic life[8]. This indicator used median rent for each community, as reported by Simply Map[9]. Median rent was compared to median income to show the proportion of income being spent on rent. Communities where a higher proportion of income is being consumed by rent have more *intensity*.

- **Population Turnover**. Using data reported by Simply Map, the level of community turnover was assessed - the higher the level of population turnover, the more intense the disadvantage. When a community has high turnover rates, the ability to be empowered to engage with a process like IWM is diminished.

- **High School Education**. This indicator suggests that when communities have a high proportion of the population without high school education, the intensity of disadvantage will be greater. This indicator will primarily speak to the character of engagement that is required.

- **Unemployment**. With greater unemployment, the intensity of disadvantage increases. A caveat is that unemployment data are variable over time; this analysis used the American Community Survey estimation of 2010 census data.

RESULTS

Each indicator was scored using equal intervals within its range of values. Each interval was given a score, and each community received the score appropriate to its place in each range. We used this simplified process of normalization during this pilot, and agree and encourage that a more rigorous method be developed during future research. By normalizing to scores, we were quickly able to plot each of the communities using the three indices.

In *Figure 3*, the size of each circle references the size of a community, with more populous communities having larger circles. The vertical axis shows the scores for uniformity, and the horizontal axis the scores for intensity. In this analysis, a large circle towards the upper right of the chart would be a high-population community with high *intensity* and high *uniformity* – meaning this community likely has greater need and engagement could have a greater impact.

This analysis was used to select the four communities assigned for outreach in the second round of engagement. The study sought communities that described a spread within the middle of the spectrum of the analysis, primarily because of the need to achieve successes within the scope of the grant budget.

Future efforts can use this assessment to help design engagement efforts when a specific community is pre-selected. This tool can also help prioritize resources, so that engagement in communities that place very low can be granted additional resources and time, and those that place highly can have their efforts scaled appropriately.

This analysis tool requires additional research and standardization. In concept it could be used throughout the urban IWM regions of California to assist engagement efforts with the residents of disadvantaged communities. Needed are a refinement of the indices and engagement with social scientists to help properly balance the selected indicators.

---

8   Ramakrishnan, S. Karthick and Mark Baldassare, 2004. *The Ties that Bind: Changing Demographics and Civic Engagement in California*. Public Policy Institute of California.

9   *http://geographicresearch.com/simplymap*

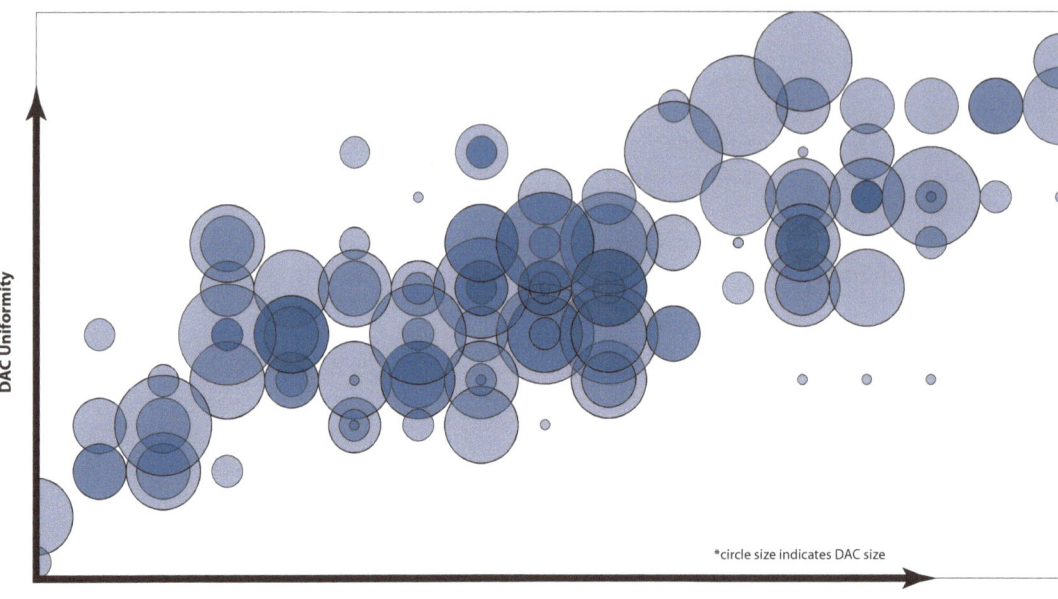

Figure 3. Plot of community scoring (normalized).

DAC Uniformity

*circle size indicates DAC size

DAC Intensity

Engagement Efforts

This Study engaged and provided technical assistance to five communities. The city of Maywood was selected as our pilot site[10] with input from the GLAC IRWM DAC Committee and the 2010 report *Hidden Hazards*[11].

The four communities selected for the second round of outreach were chosen using the boundary-setting and multi-indicator analyses described above. The communities were selected so that one was in each of the four subregions of GLAC-IRWM that contain DAC tracts and further refined for effective engagement *(Figure 5)*.

- **Long Beach:** Eastside

- **City of Gardena:** Northeast side

- **Greater El Monte:** south of Interstate 10 & northern South El Monte

- **Greater North Hollywood:** Northeast side

As the pilot outreach in Maywood has already been described, the next section will focus on the main outreach effort in these four communities.

---

10   Details about the Maywood pilot project are found at: *http://wc.watershedhealth.org*

11   *http://www.libertyhill.org/document.doc?id=202*

Outreach Contractors

For the main engagement activity, Study staff and disadvantaged community committee members selected three outreach contractors to perform four community engagements. Each contractor was given two months and a $25,000 budget to develop the needs assessment for the assigned community.

Outreach contractors were selected for their knowledge of IWM principles (but not necessarily process) and experience with innovative forms of outreach. These criteria were different than that used in the Maywood pilot and were informed by lessons learned during the pilot. For Maywood, the contractor was selected because of local knowledge and an existing network of engaged community members. This allowed the contractor to engage with many people, however, it also caused them miss sectors of the community with which they don't normally engage. For the main outreach engagement, the selection criteria focused on innovation and adaptation characteristics in contractors.

Outreach contractors followed the needs assessment framework to describe IWM-related needs of communities, to coordinate with the Study team to improve the needs assessment framework, and to engage with technical consultants to help develop projects. By design of the selection team, the three contractors varied in experience, knowledge and

Figure 5. IRWM Regions and Selected Communities Map

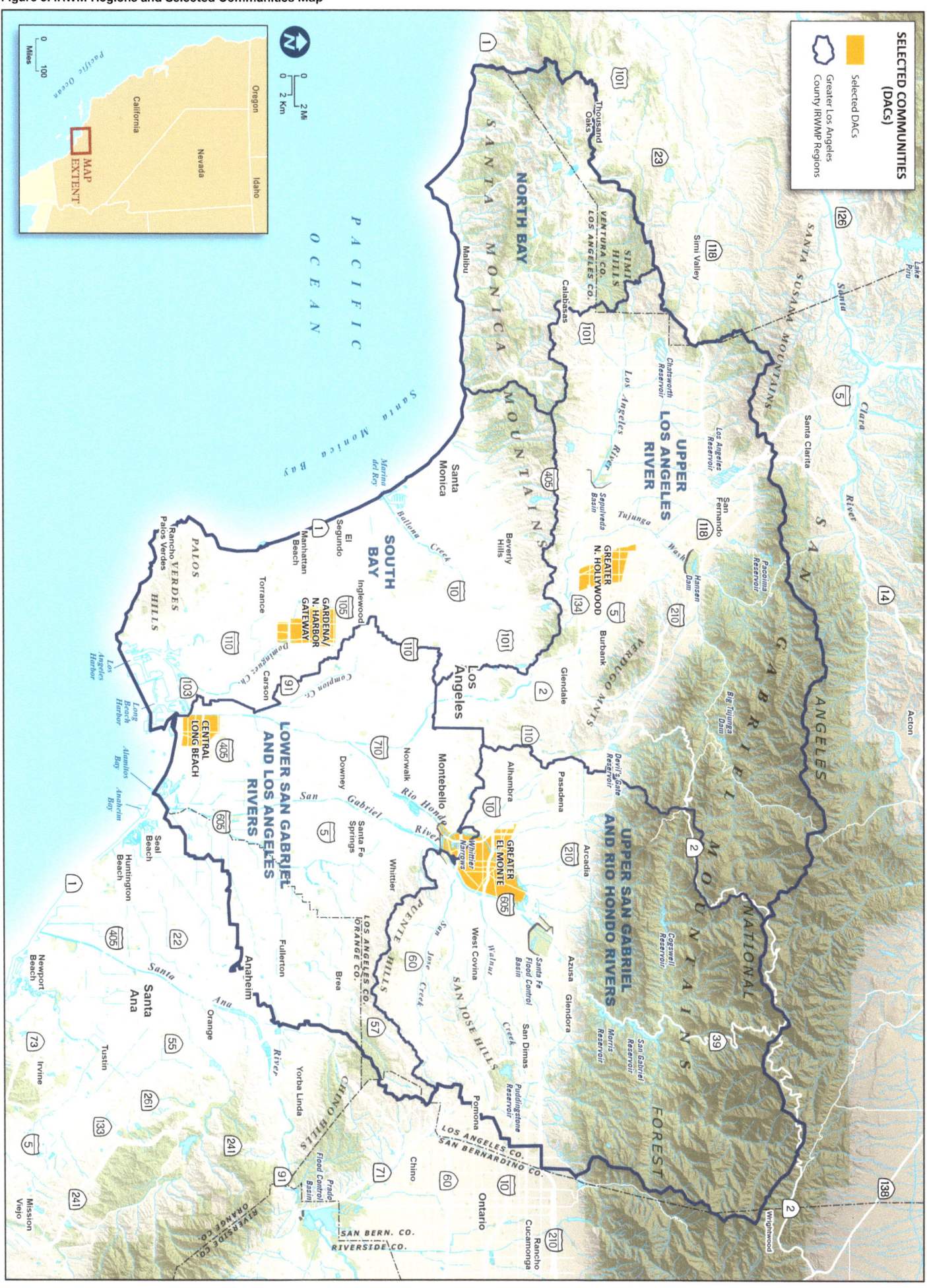

approach. One was a grassroots nonprofit that is successful in building support for parks and open space projects in disadvantaged communities. Another was a public affairs for-profit consultant that frequently contracts with large agencies to do outreach related to large public works projects. The third was a small urban planning and public process for-profit consultant headed by a technical expert on IRWM.

Technical Assistance

At the end of the engagement effort, the Council brought in two technical consultant teams to develop project concepts for inclusion in the GLAC-IRWM database of potential projects. The Los Angeles Flood Control District, via an agreement with the US Army Corps of Engineers *Planning Assistance to the States* program, provided one of the technical consultants. The second technical consultant was selected in a competitive process similar to that which selected the outreach contractors.

Outreach contractors interacted with the technical consultants through the Study to flesh out ideas. Project concepts were shared back to the community for comments and further developed. Out of twenty-two project concepts, eight received technical assistance *(Table 2)*. Two of the projects receiving technical assistance are in Maywood. Project concept reports and documents about each of these projects are available at: http://wc.watershedhealth.org.

Table 2. Project concepts for the GLAC-IRWM database.

	Project Title	Project Organization	Received Technical Assistance
1	Northeast Gardena Recycled Water Line	West Basin Municipal Water District	
2	Vermont Median Stormwater Park	Council for Watershed Health	Y
3	Rehabilitate 2,000,000 Gallon Water Tank	Maywood Mutual Water Company #1	Y
4	Maywood Mutual Water Company #2: Build 2nd Manganese Treatment Plant	Maywood Mutual Water Company #2	Y
5	Gray Water Standard Implementation	City of Long Beach (submitted by Gateway IRWM for Prop 84 Round 2 Funding)	Y
6	Maywood Mutual Water Company #2: Repair Mainlines and Eliminate System Dead-Ends	Maywood Mutual Water Company #2	
7	Maywood Mutual Water Company #1: Install Street Valves and Eliminate System Dead-Ends	Maywood Mutual Water Company #1	
8	Maywood Mutual Water Company #1: Replace 25% of Mainlines in System	Maywood Mutual Water Company #1	
9	Maywood Mutual Water Company #1: Manganese Filter Installation	Maywood Mutual Water Company #1	
10	Maywood Mutual Water Company #1: 500,000 Gallon Water Tank	Maywood Mutual Water Company #1	
11	SEMOU Groundwater Plan Scoping	San Gabriel Basin Water Quality Authority	
12	Maywood Mutual Water Company #3: Tank Relining	Maywood Mutual Water Company #3	
13	Maywood Mutual Water Company #3: Rehabilitate/ Replace Mainlines	Maywood Mutual Water Company #3	
14	Maywood Mutual Water Company #3: TCE Treatment Plant (if required)	Maywood Mutual Water Company #3	
15	Maywood Mutual Water Company #3: New Water Well	Maywood Mutual Water Company #3	
16	SEMOU Groundwater Treatment and Remediation	San Gabriel Basin Water Quality Authority	
17	Northeast Gardena Storm Water Quality Park, Recycled Water Line, and Landscape Makeover	Council for Watershed Health	
18	North Hollywood Groundwater and Surface Water Benefits Study	Council for Watershed Health	Y
19	North Hollywood Transmission Corridor Easement Stormwater Capture Study	Council for Watershed Health	Y
20	Northeast Gardena Water and Landscape Makeover, Community Involvement Module	Council for Watershed Health	
21	Garvey Avenue Stormwater Quality Streetscape Retrofit	Council for Watershed Health	Y
22	North Hollywood Street Enhancement	City of Los Angeles	Y

LESSONS LEARNED

Below are general lessons learned summarized from the five engagement efforts.

Scale of Engagement: Size Matters

Properly understanding the character of a disadvantaged community aids efforts to engage with its members. This study reinforces the need to engage in precise and small-area communities, as it is there that communities are able to make collective decisions. Further, small-scale engagement projects can succeed on nominal budgets.

Initially, communities identified by the Study team were much too large and populous, making it difficult to effectively engage with the relatively small budget allocated to each effort. In recognition of this issue, the Council allowed Outreach Contractors to focus on a subset area of each community.

Identifying the proper scale of engagement to reach a community but also develop projects that are appropriately sized is critical and should be part of the analysis prior to engagement activities begin.

Key Problems Identified by Needs Assessment

The critical IWM-related needs of urban disadvantaged communities are related to flood risk management, surface water quality, and open space provisioning. Though in some cases delivered water quality was raised as a challenge, community members never suggested that sanitation was a problem.

Below summarizes the challenges most frequently mentioned by community members during engagement efforts of this study.

FLOODING
Flooding is usually of concern in communities that suffer from *local* flooding. Urban surface flooding that impacts pedestrians and traffic was raised on several occasions. The potential for region-wide flooding during major storm events was not something the communities were aware of, and didn't prioritize it during engagement.

DRINKING WATER QUALITY
The drinking water quality challenges in an urban context are magnified by the number of people who are impacted and by the institutional density (water provider, water wholesaler, groundwater authority, etc.). In GLAC-IRWM region the drinking water quality concern comes from small water providers who draw groundwater that is high in manganese. Manganese is not a health issue, *per se*, but does cause discoloration and odor. People perceive that discolored, smelly water must be unhealthful; assertions by authorities that the water is safe to drink have created an atmosphere of distrust. The water does stain laundry and is unpleasant to bathe in.

IWM is the right governance model for engaging with these challenges, however, the institutions that suffer these challenges struggle to participate in IWM for lack of staff and limited budgets.

SURFACE WATER QUALITY
No community member in the focus communities expressed concerns about surface water quality. With adoption of the new MS4 permit for Los Angeles County, cities and unincorporated LA County are now working to solve stormwater pollution. That none of the people engaged by this study recognized this challenge speaks to the disconnection between people and streams in Greater LA County.

The impact of poor stormwater quality is primarily indirect; that is, stormwater quality regulations will require expenditures by municipalities and

Table 3. Park open space acreage by focus community.

Focus Community	Park Space Acreage per 1,000 persons*
Maywood	0.27
North Hollywood	0.56
Greater El Monte	0.00
Long Beach	0.15
Gardena	0.81

* Acreage calculated by selecting the centroid of the output project concepts from the Council's outreach and using the California State Parks website "Community FactFinder" Available: *http://www.parkinfo.org/factfinder2011/grantee*

the County, affecting the ability of those governments to provide other services. The impact of poor stormwater quality isn't seen as having a direct impact, health related or not, on community members. This lack of direct impact remains a challenge for funding projects. IWM is the right governance mechanism for resolving this challenge, as it will pursue multiple-benefit projects that bring necessary stormwater quality benefits.

OPEN SPACE

On average, park open space in the focus communities was well below the accepted standard of four acres of open space per 1,000 persons *(Table 3)*. Despite each of the focus areas being quite dense and lacking parks and open space, however, there was no great concern expressed specifically about the lack of open space. There was, however, a great deal of concern about community beautification and proper maintenance of those parks that do exist.

TRANSPORTATION NETWORK

In four of the five efforts the community drew attention to the transportation infrastructure. Complaints ranged from lack of safe and shaded sidewalks to degraded road surfaces to high rates of speed on the streets. IWM cannot directly respond to these problems, however, roads carry stormwater by design and a roadway retrofit in this region could include green infrastructure to benefit water supply and water quality. Three of the proposed projects incorporated the community's call for improved roads with green street or median parkway proposals.

Outreach Strategies Used In This Study

Each of the engagement strategies used by the outreach contractors and the study team were effective in specific settings; in general, however, success came from a blending of multiple techniques. When outreach contractors struggled, we determined that it was because the strategy selected was not working. Key to success is the ability to be flexible and adaptive in the use of engagement strategies.

TALKING TO THE COMMUNITY

"Sidewalk Engagements". When standard community meetings failed to attract enough participants, outreach contractors set up shop with some coffee and donuts in the focus area. It

became clear, however, that high pedestrian traffic areas should be targeted for this type of outreach or more staff time budgeted in lower traffic areas; this type of outreach required patience and time. This strategy selects site users, so it was useful to employ the strategy after a site was selected.

Neighborhood Canvasing. Neighborhood canvassing provided a great deal of community context. Even though formal meeting or survey input wasn't collected, offhand comments made by residents—even reasons why residents didn't want to talk—provided useful input about how people felt their city could improve related to water-resources.

Brief Surveys (less than three minutes). One contractor engaged a youth group to distribute over three hundred paper surveys to community members. The surveys did not mention IWM specifically, instead asking people to respond to questions about drinking water, open space, and storm water/flooding issues, as well as their neighborhoods more generally. The surveys were most useful in identifying how community members think about water, and can be used to target follow-up engagement activities.

Long-Form Interviews. In several of the communities, outreach contractors discovered that there were no active groups of community members. In the absence of existing groups, finding a communication path to these communities is a significant challenge, especially for agencies, which are often either invisible to or distrusted by the residents. In one such community, the contractor observed a large number of Laundromats and judged that these would be good spots for long-form interviews. They reasoned that the Laundromats would serve the lowest income members of the community and that those residents would be available for an interview during the laundry cycle. They sent Spanish-speaking interviewers, who offered $50 Target Gift Cards as compensation for those willing to participate ($30 gift cards would likely achieve the same results). These interviews were very successful.

Institutional Stakeholder Interviews (businesses, institutions). This technique was very successful. In this step the outreach contractor would engage with institutions (schools, civic centers, businesses, religious institutions) to help identify where the most civically active members of the community gather, and work to engage them in the conversation. These groups often could identify peers that would otherwise have been overlooked, and could also leverage their networks to assure that community members become engaged with the effort.

One contractor described their process:
We started researching stakeholders by searching online to find what organizations are either located in, or have jurisdiction in, the community. We formed a long list of these organizations and narrowed down to the top 20 that we wanted to interview further. While we were conducting these interviews we used the Snowball Sampling method to find who the "Active Community Members" in the area really are. In this method the interviewer asks each point of contact to recommend another point of contact to interview who is knowledgeable in the subject matter. This system of referrals identifies the network structure within a community for a given issue. This is called the snowball method because we accumulate information about the network as we go, like a snowball accumulates more snow as it rolls down hill. It will provide an additional layer of feedback about the stakeholders we have already identified and test whether or not the entities we think play the most active role in our study area actually do.

This combination of research and an expanding circle of interviews were very useful in uncovering the most significant needs in the community.

Focus Groups. One contractor assembled focus groups. Using existing senior and youth groups, the contractor made presentations about the region, and IWM generally, and sought ideas and concepts from the gathered groups. In this short-term group activity, the outreach contractor found that the participants were not able to contribute meaningfully. They struggled to place their ideas inside the target community (not all participants were from that community), and as was discovered elsewhere, the complexity of the IWM system is off-putting to community members in presentation form.

PARTNERING
Municipal Agency Meetings
Meetings with municipal agencies were successful. Facilitating a meeting between the outreach contractors, the Council for Watershed Health,

and the relevant municipal agency representatives was always an important step. Municipal agency members are cautious when nonprofits begin speaking with community members, wary that expectations will be improperly or unrealistically raised. Describing the engagement effort, and learning how the municipal staff understands the challenges facing the community must be part of any community engagement effort.

Adapting Water-Related Needs From Prior Outreach. In one of the outreach regions, a local foundation, the California Endowment, had conducted general outreach about community needs and produced a report. The Study team used that document to describe IWM-related needs. This example of aligning engagement with existing or recent efforts is another important strategy.

Partnering With Local Non-profits. One contractor partnered with two local nonprofit groups. The partnerships were productive, permitting the outreach contractor to reach significantly more residents of the community, as well as municipal agency representatives. Leveraging existing engaged groups is one of the hallmarks of the needs assessment framework, and in this case it was proven very successful.

EDUCATION
Water Resource Facility Tour. One contractor partnered with a local water resources agency to give a tour to members of two local nonprofit groups. This tour, which relied on water education materials developed by the agency, was highly effective in capturing the interest of regular community members and their organizations. The tour generated much discussion and was related to the ultimate project concept that was developed in Long Beach.

Explicitly Describing the IRWM Program in Detail and Requesting Input at Community Meetings. This strategy was not successful. Two main problems were encountered. First, it proved very difficult to draw an audience of community members when the purpose of the meeting was advertised as "learning about integrated water management". Each time the Council, outreach contractors or technical contractors convened a meeting where the purpose was education about water attendance was very low.

Second, the complexity of IWM is nearly impossible to share quickly and effectively with a lay audience. Efforts to do so caused confusion, boredom, or simply left participants unclear on how their voices could be valuable.

Comic Book. One contractor worked with youth to develop a comic book that described IWM from the perspective of an alien visiting Southern California from another planet. The comic was produced in the three most commonly spoken languages in the community (Khmer, Spanish, and English). The Council recommends formally evaluating the comic book to determine its usefulness educating people just beginning to learn about water resources.

Mobile Water Education Station. The panels from the comic book were installed on a mobile panel board that was displayed at a community event. The display generated significant attention during the event. For this reason, we conclude an information station that can be moved around the community is a good engagement strategy.

SPECIFIC FINDINGS IN SELECTED COMMUNITIES

Each of the communities we engaged displayed different levels of pre-existing involvement in civic issues in general and IWM in particular *(Table 4)*. The project team found that Maywood and Long Beach both had high levels of existing activity. Maywood had existing outreach and advocacy activity carried out by the same organization that was selected as our outreach contractor. In Long Beach, the California Endowment has invested for a long period of time and we found many thriving organizations and ongoing conversations. It was unquestionably easier to work in Long Beach and Maywood because of these organizing efforts—it was easy to identify the community's primary concerns.

The remaining three communities were lacking any existing groups or conversations. In Greater El Monte, a great deal of community organizing has been done in the past, but has been dormant for a long period of time. Greater North Hollywood has links to the North Hollywood Arts District, but is itself lacking any coherent civic engagement. Gardena has a strong city government that handles

Table 4. Variation in DACs.

DAC	Civic Activity	Water Knowledge
Maywood	High	High
Long Beach	High	Low
El Monte	Low	Low
N. Hollywood	Low	Low
Gardena	Low	Low

most of the communications with the community. The outreach contractor struggled to access that existing communication channel and the City was unable to respond within the short timeline of the outreach. In the end, however, the city of Gardena was a strong partner during project concept development.

The following table *(Table 5)* briefly summarizes the needs expressed most clearly by the communities during the engagement process, and our brief proposals of next steps for developing additional projects in that community.

Table 5. Feedback of Community Needs and Proposals for Solutions

DAC	NEEDS	PROPOSALS
Maywood	• A perception that their water delivery infrastructure is aging and contributes to drinking water quality compliance issues. • A perception that water is too expensive. • Frustration that there are few or no regulatory tools to address the water quality issues of concern stemming from elevated levels of manganese, which is not classified as a primary constituent or regulated.	• Support improvements to each of the three mutual water companies to ensure continued low levels of Manganese in the drinking water. • Help the three mutual water companies replace aging infrastructure. • Offer facilitation services for the three mutual water companies and for surrounding water companies in the region to explore integrated solutions and management. • Offer programs to residents to cost-effectively reduce consumption through plumbing and landscape retrofits.
Long Beach	• Lack of open space. This community is among those in the region without sufficient green recreational space for the number of people living there. • Reliability of imported water. Community members had knowledge of water conservation and water reuse, but felt insufficiently supported by water agencies.	• Work with regional open space advocates and city government to consider additional parks that provide additional water benefits. • Assist the City of Long Beach Office of Sustainability in expanding their Laundry to Landscape graywater program into other graywater applications and into more dense housing types.
El Monte	• Groundwater contamination in El Monte is currently being remediated by the San Gabriel Valley Water Quality Authority, an active member of the GLAC-IRWM group. • Cross-boundary government collaboration. The community we engaged straddles between two municipalities with the boundary running down the middle of Garvey Avenue. Because the roadway and community is managed by two government structures, the community believes that it receives fewer resources.	• Work to bring more resources to the groundwater basin remediation project underway at the San Gabriel Water Quality Authority. • Use watershed coordinators to engage El Monte and South El Monte in joint planning and project proposals to fund projects in the boundary community and along Garvey Avenue. • Help the Upper San Gabriel Valley Municipal Water District expand its network of recycled water lines.
North Hollywood	• Localized flooding. Much of this area of the San Fernando Valley, due to low slopes and extensive development, suffers surface flooding during storms. • Groundwater contamination. The eastern San Fernando Basin, which underlies this community, has legacy aerospace pollution plumes. Los Angeles Department of Water and Power and the EPA Superfund program are both working to mitigate this pollution. • Lack of open space. Community members asked for beautification of their neighborhood.	• Work to bring more resources to the groundwater basin remediation efforts. • Link sustainable development practices into general plan and transportation improvements.
Gardena	High Water Costs • The city of Gardena struggles to keep traditionally-landscaped public space irrigated. • Residential bills straining family budgets. Lack of Open Space • Insufficient park space for the population. • An historic wetland that is closed on all but one day of each month because there is no funding to staff the site or build visitor's amenities.	• Offer assistance to West Basin Municipal Water District and the City of Gardena in expanding its network of recycled water lines • Encourage retrofits of public space landscapes with native plants that require less irrigation. • Offer programs to residents to reduce the water used for household uses and irrigation.

FINDINGS APPLICABLE THROUGHOUT URBAN AREAS OF CALIFORNIA

The following findings are applicable throughout the IWM process in California where disadvantaged community engagement is attempted. These concepts are particularly relevant for urban areas.

The study resulted in findings and recommendations for improving the engagement of members of disadvantaged communities, specifically for urban areas but which are also likely applicable statewide.

Indicators of Disadvantage and Critical Needs

Properly identifying and understanding a disadvantaged community greatly improves efforts to engage with its members. The use of the median-household income statistic has utility, however it is not sufficient when developing an engagement strategy that relies on awareness of a community's individuality. We concluded that urban and rural disadvantaged communities often have different critical needs within the IWM scope and must be considered using different metrics.

If the use of "critical needs" remains in the grant guidelines for IWM in future funding efforts, we suggest the following additional indicators be used to identify disadvantaged communities for urban IWM regions: Size of the community, Intensity and Uniformity of the challenges faced by the community.

Recommendation. DWR invests in research to enhance and expand the tools described herein to provide IWM groups with the information necessary to properly identify community boundaries and to help understand the uniformity and intensity of the disadvantage experienced by each community.

Investment in Communities: Using the Right People for the Job

Engagement requires particular skills and the investment of both time and money. Funding directed towards people and organizations with necessary skills is required for IWM agencies to conduct effective and sustainable disadvantaged community engagement.

So too, the organizations hired to perform engagement work should have some awareness of IWM or have worked with regional planning authorities in the past. This knowledge will permit them to more easily connect the community's needs to the capacity of the IRWM program and agencies.

Of the four outreach contractors engaged in this study, for example, one had significant IWM experience and staff that were well-trained in urban planning principles. While each of our engagements was effective in different ways appropriate to each community, we found that this contractor communicated more effectively with IWM institutions than contractors without these skills and knowledge.

Recommendation. DWR uses grant guidelines to create a set-aside, perhaps up to 10 percent, within planning grants for engagement activities. Grantees should enunciate an engagement plan to access these targeted planning funds and the resources used to assure disadvantaged community members are able to participate in IWM planning efforts.

Orienting Towards Results: Flexibility

Members of disadvantaged communities and the organizations most able to engage on water issues struggle to use state grant funds themselves because of the long period between incurring an expense and receiving reimbursement. To overcome this challenge, we provided our outreach contractors up-front money to permit them to accomplish tasks they were otherwise unable to perform for lack of operating funds. Without this "advance," they would have been unable to perform as effectively, for lack of operating funds. A similar system of flexibility in the funding set-aside for disadvantage community engagement efforts is necessary.

Recommendation. DWR makes it easier for small agencies and organizations to conduct this work through expedited reimbursement and small up-front funding grants.

State Agency Alignment: DOC Watershed Coordinators Integrate

Council for Watershed Health has operated a Department of Conservation Watershed Coordinator Grant for the past eight years and until recently was able to fund an additional watershed coordinator through a number of different grants. With this experience, we have seen that the work of watershed coordinators and the work of disadvantaged community outreach, at least in urban southern California, are very similar.

Among our successes in this study were the building of partnerships with and between local governments, agencies and community groups *(Table 6)*. Many of these stakeholders were not previously engaged with IWM. In most cases, our work created new links between IWM agencies and other organizations that were new to the effort.

DWR and IWM would benefit by aligning with the California Department of Conservation to provide additional resources, goals, and agency support for the Watershed Coordination Program focused in IWM areas. By strengthening the Watershed Coordination Program DWR could leverage a successful and existing program to provide benefits to urban DAC.

Recommendation. DWR works with DOC to strengthen and expand the Watershed Coordination Program in highly-urbanized areas to leverage a successful and existing program, which is currently underfunded and understaffed.

Critical Needs in Highly Urban Communities

Urban and rural disadvantaged communities often have different critical needs within the IWM scope and must be considered using different metrics. No critical need is "more" than another; instead each is unique to the context of a particular community. Our work often came down to seeing if one of the GLAC-IRWM priorities could properly address needs identified by a community. Instead, the community's needs must be engaged when setting the priorities.

IWM Planning grants must direct funding for effective disadvantaged community engagement, just as implementation grants set-aside resources for DAC projects. At the moment DAC members are engaged during the project concept phase of IWM and are not provided tools, resources or opportunities to engage when the IWM plans are being formulated. With DWR's desire to have local priorities drive the effort, we need to assure that

Table 6. Stakeholder Engagement Successes

DAC	ENTITIES NOT PREVIOUSLY INVOLVED IN DAC	ENTITIES PREVIOUSLY INVOLVED IN DAC
Maywood	Union de Vecinos Maywood Mutual Water Company #1 Maywood Mutual Water Company #2 Maywood Inter-Agency Partnership • EJ Network • US EPA • CA Department of Toxic Substances Control	Water Replenishment District of Southern California
Long Beach	United Cambodian Community Catalyst City of Long Beach Office of Sustainability	The City of Long Beach and the Long Beach Water Department are members of the Gateway IRWM
El Monte	Club Durazo The Janet Chin Foundation City of El Monte City of South El Monte	Upper San Gabriel Valley Water District San Gabriel Basin Water Quality Authority
North Hollywood	MCC In the Valley Church North Hollywood Neighborhood Council	Los Angeles Department of Water and Power
Gardena	City of Gardena From Lot to Spot	West Basin Municipal Water District City of Los Angeles

all communities are provided opportunity to help create the local priorities.

Examples of critical needs identified in urban Greater Los Angeles included:

- *Flooding* - age and sufficiency of flood risk management infrastructure

- *Water Services* - The number and size of customer base of water companies relative to community population

- *Green Open Space* - Access to parks that is not blocked by physical and cultural boundaries, such as freeways and gang territories

- *Clean Water* - Amount of (area and linear miles) impaired surface water bodies.

Recommendation. DWR broadens its guidance on 'critical needs' to include the water-related challenges of urban disadvantaged communities including: drinking water quality, stormwater quality, and lack of open space.

Inclusiveness and Sensitivity: Words are Important

Two aspects of language provided significant lessons. First, in the GLAC-IRWM region many disadvantaged community members are not native English speakers. To engage, both verbal and written communication needed to be made in the language of the community. This requirement is both necessary and respectful.

In the technical assistance efforts led by the Army Corps of Engineers, both the Study team and the Army Corps worked to assure that project concept reports were translated.

Second, the concept of "disadvantaged community" is a powerful tool in policy documents, California Codes, and bond language. Care must be taken during engagement with people so that their lived experience is acknowledged and respected. The reductionist nature of the name (and particularly the pronounced acronym "Dacks") can work to reaffirm barriers and differences between the parties in an engagement.

Recommendation. DWR works with social scientists and community members to develop conscientious language and guidance that improves the inclusiveness and sensitivity of engagement efforts.

STRATEGIES FOR ENGAGEMENT

A community-capacity based engagement model was derived from the experiences of this study. In this model, we propose three approaches for interaction between IWM and disadvantaged communities. They are listed from the greatest to the least degree of existing community engagement capacity:

1. Community-Led Engagement

2. IWM Institution-Led Project Outreach

3. IWM Institution-Led Community Needs

This model is generalizable to work anywhere in California. The Department of Water Resources can use it to tune grant guidelines that encourage effective engagement efforts, and local IWM planning work can use it to assure that all communities in their region are playing a role in selecting priorities and projects.

In the model, an "IWM institution" includes any of the government agencies, joint-powers-authorities, state conservancies, or NGOs that take part in the formal IWM governance, or water resources or land management more generally. Similarly, the "community" in the model can be made up of individual residents, neighborhood groups, municipal representatives, or community-based NGOs (or a combination of these).

Community-Led Engagement

In this type of engagement, the community comes together on its own, identifies their perceived needs and project interests, and seeks out the IWM institution to help ensure implementation. All that is required of the IWM institution is to be open, accessible and receptive. This model is the least common in disadvantaged communities, primarily because they rarely have the necessary community organizing capacity in place. Often a local nonprofit or foundation can be enlisted to overcome this deficit by generating this level of engagement. Either way, under this approach the role of the IWM institution is to take action to become open and available to hear the community when it asks for help. There are many ways to accomplish this, for instance, adding staff with community affairs or community liaison duties, robust advertising,

listening sessions, and social-network feeds. IWM institutions must realign their structures to achieve openness, and to become more available when the community attempts to reach out.

IWM Institution-Led Project Outreach

This type of engagement is suited for when an IWM institution has a project that is already advancing through the design and funding process, but has not been vetted with the community. That institution can use the tools provided in this engagement approach to establish which communities will be impacted by the project, and how to properly design an engagement process that will notify the community of the project and seek input in its implementation. This is closest to the traditional outreach model, which could be considered the "notification" model. Notification alone is not sufficient because it only pushes information out, which has no impact on the project itself. The engagement work for this approach requires both pushing project and technical information out to the community, but then also proactively obtaining and pulling community feedback information back into the project development process.

Institution-Led Community Needs Assessments

This type of engagement is suited for areas where institutions have no IWM projects identified, and the communities do not have the capacity to identify them on their own. In this type of engagement, an IWM institution engages with the disadvantaged community to investigate and document the full range of social, economic, physical and environmental community needs, without a specific water-related project concept in mind. In this engagement specialists should be brought in to work with the community on this needs assessment. Local NGO's and universities can be valuable contractors here. Once that is done, the institution and its technical contractors work with the community to identify IWM related project opportunities that will best suit the local conditions and community needs that were identified.

The outreach and technical assistance of this Study was consistent with this engagement approach.

CONCLUSIONS

Integrated water management fundamentally seeks the engagement of all those who have a stake in water and land resources. Bringing members of low-income communities into the process requires investments of time and money, and skills that are not always possessed by institutions of water and land management. Specific actions and policy can improve the engagement of community members in IWM.

This report describes an effort to bring the members of disadvantaged communities in the Greater Los Angeles County region into the IWM project selection process. This study produced tools and strategies that can be used to enhance the effort to engage disadvantaged communities.

Properly identifying a community, and understanding the challenges that community faces, must be first steps in an engagement effort. Thus the first step in our outreach process, after identifying the target communities, was to conduct a needs assessment. Institutions must invest time and money in becoming available to community-led engagement and pursuing engagement when appropriate through needs assessments and project and planning scoping processes.

Appropriate engagement doesn't stop with awareness. There must be a purpose to the engagement. Community members must feel that not only were their concerns heard, they were responded to in a way that was congruent with their needs. All to often, agencies are perceived as asking questions to provide cover for a project already underway. Thus it is important that IWM institutions augment their abilities and improve their approaches to engaging with members of the communities they serve. Department of Water Resources can use grant guidelines to assure that members of disadvantaged communities are sufficiently engaged during IWM goal-setting, project planning, and project implementation.

Effective engagement with members of disadvantaged communities during IWM planning and project selection can provide much-needed benefits to those communities. There are critical needs faced by urban disadvantaged communities within the scope of IWM, though these needs have thus far not been recognized by DWR or the regional IWM effort.

The disadvantaged communities of Greater Los Angeles County have specific needs related to IWM and will benefit greatly from more effective engagement activities that capture those needs during IWM planning. This report has shown how GLAC-IRWM can accomplish greater engagement, to the benefit of the people living and working in the region. Department of Water Resources, using these findings, will be able to steer regional IWM towards more successful engagement outcomes.

APPENDIX

Contractor List

Contractor	Emphasis/Experience
Union de Vecinos (Pilot Program contractor)	Build healthy and viable communities through improving housing and environmental conditions in Boyle Heights and Maywood. The organization has been embedded in Maywood since 2006.
From Lot to Spot	Improve green space and quality of life in low-income neighborhoods. Stimulate and contribute to community economic development in blighted communities. The organization has worked across the region in low-income communities since 2006.
Connective Issue	Environmental consulting firm focused on watershed management and water use. The firm works across the region and was founded in 2007.
The Sierra Group	Public relations firm focused on balancing business goals and community needs. The firm works across the region and was founded in 1993.

www.ingramcontent.com/pod-product-compliance
Lightning Source LLC
Chambersburg PA
CBHW060820290526
45792CB00005BB/1731